"I've read a lot of books. But I've never read a book quite like this one. And you haven't either. I've also written a bunch of books. But none like this. However, a unique book is just a novelty if it's not also a meaningful book. And Kelly Collins has written a profoundly meaningful book. Honest, raw, and deep, Collins has woven her story in with the interviews and stories of fellow pilgrims, and together the textures and rich colors of these deeply personal narratives make an extraordinary tapestry.

Renowned spiritual writer, Frederick Buechner, said that the reason he had written and published his memoir was because 'I'm convinced that the story of any one of us is to some degree the story of us all.' One of the treasures of this book is how many of the experiences and emotions will feel familiar because pain, resilience, and recovery are recurring themes in your story also.

And ultimately that's why this book matters—because it's really about your story, especially the chapters yet to be written, chapters you'll be writing with a new perspective, chapters about a painful but redeemed past, a presently transformed life, and a future waiting to be kissed square on the lips."

—**Ramon Presson,** *PhD, licensed therapist and author of When Will My Life Not Suck? Authentic Hope for the Disillusioned*

"Reading 'The Swipe Right Effect' will likely encourage self-examination and growth. While the following words may sound trite, they are sure to resonate with readers, when Collins writes, 'You can always find a lesson to learn from. What is also true is that if you don't put yourself out there, you might not learn, you might not grow and you might not find what you need. It's hard to fail, but it is harder to get to what you truly want without these lessons or without trying.' After completing the book, one understands why the back cover describes it as 'the moon reflecting the love light of others.'"

—Lucie-Anne Dionne-Thomas,
Newport This Week Book Review

"Through her openness in sharing the universal emotion of pain, Kelly captures real life examples and solutions which are transferrable to every human being. Each personal story gives a spark of hope that there is a path through pain. As you read each chapter, you gain the awareness that you are not alone in your story. The exercises at the end of each chapter provide insight on how to move through as well as into your next chapter in life with greater peace and grace."

—Allison Morgan, *MA, OTR, E-RYT,*
CEO of Zensational Kids

"If this book has found its way to you, take a moment and look around. Remember who you are and what your outlook on life, love and loss is. Then start reading. You will not be the same person after reading this book that you are now.

You are about to meet your new best friend, Kelly, and she is going to introduce you to some amazing women. Strong, Soft and Smart women who will never leave you. Your story and their stories will weave in and out of each other until wisdom, mercy, self-acceptance and gratitude are more real to you than ever before.

It would take three or four lifetimes to experience all the wisdom these stories contain. Yet, here it is. In one book- through one woman's adventures into living life wholeheartedly."

—**Reverend Caren Teichmann,** *M.Div, Lead Pastor*

"A fabulous read about one woman's healing journey after her divorce. Told in a series of interviews with 10 different women, the interviews discuss topics like anger, forgiveness, grief, courage, perseverance, vulnerability, and the importance of finding community in the aftermath.

She offers the reader a chance to get 'unstuck' through exercises outlined at the end of each chapter such as writing the resume of your life, defining the struggle, creating a vision board of what you want in life going forward, forgiving yourself and your former partner, and how to channel your most extroverted self and get out there to meet other like-minded people.

Collins says she is merely retelling the stories of others but she offers so much more. Intensely vulnerable, Collins shares the emotional pain she felt at that time in her life. By sharing she lets the readers know they are not alone in their experiences. A great resource!"

—S.B. Spencer

The Swipe Right Effect

WORKBOOK

C.K. COLLINS

First Edition, January 2023

Authored by: C.K. Collins
Paperback ISBN: 979-8-9876089-3-7
Hardcover ISBN: 979-8-9876089-4-4
Website: ckcollins.co

"If you have the ability to love, love yourself first."

—Charles Bukowski

CONTRACT WITH ME

BEHAVIOR CHANGE GOAL

Please place your initials by each commitment.

I agree to:

Complete the exercises in the workbook __________

Attend weekly meetings with my coach __________

Attend group support meetings __________

My goal is to complete the program by __________

In order to help me do this I am going to arrange my physical and social environment by __________

And control my internal environment by:

Meditation __________

Mindfulness __________

Reaching out for help if needed __________

CONTENTS

"Rock bottom became the solid foundation on which I rebuilt my life."

—J.K. Rowling

1

Before You Get Going

In ***The Swipe Right Effect*** book, Loretta shared with us that she self-soothes by going to her 'workshop,' which is the name she has given her safe space. It's actually quite a lovely space in her home. She has a rocking chair in front of her fireplace and the chair faces away from her desk where she sits to get her job done.

She can have a book waiting on her or have her Audible version of *The Secret* ready to listen to. This is where she can focus on her healing and her personal development.

Do you have a safe place where you can workshop an idea? If this term is not familiar to you, I will elaborate.

According to the Collins Dictionary, a **workshop** *is a period of discussion or practical work on a particular subject in which a group of people share their knowledge or experience.*

It can also mean *a seminar or series of meetings for intensive study, work, discussion, etc. in some field.*

You will be creating tangible items with which you can reflect on and work on as the weeks go by. As you are reading these chapters, there will be items that spark an interest or an idea that makes you uncomfortable. Pay attention to how you are uncomfortable and those sparks. Both are there to invite you to go deeper where you can find healing and hope.

EMPOWERMENT PRACTICE 1: FIND YOUR DREAM WORKSHOP

It's important you find your workshop as we dive into working together. You will require a quiet place to meditate and work through some hard memories and situations.

Can you find a place where you can have a candle, a water bottle, your favorite journal and pen? A blanket and cushion to sit on while meditating might be helpful. Soft lighting would be preferable as you want to be in a calm state and relaxed while you workshop.

Here are some steps you can follow to prepare:

Identify Your Physical Workshop

This will be a place that makes you feel safe where you can have privacy to think through ideas. If you don't have that privacy in your home, consider getting a study room at a library, find a park bench, or seek out a chapel at a church. We all need a peaceful place to ponder our next steps when life is providing us challenges.

Whereas exercise provides an outlet for letting out bad energy and creating new, better energy, what I'm suggesting for your workshop space is to be still. Be still and listen to your heart. Know that you are healing. Be still and follow your instincts.

Display Your Work to Review

Keep your workbook and journal and other creatives in this safe place. Regularly review what you have written, look at your vision board and review your Life Purpose resume. Look back at these items. Are there changes you want to make? There should be an evolving of how you see these works. It will be exciting when you have a breakthrough and want to make changes.

Although workshops are sometimes a group exercise, this workshop is for you to do "*practical work on a particular subject*" as the definition suggests. Tackle your doubts, your insecurities, your anger and anything else that is a block for your good energy. My hope is that in being still and confronting these blocks, you will accelerate your healing.

Listen to those subtle hints your body will give you. Like Loretta, follow what your inside voice is telling you.

Prepare for Meditation

Meditation will be practiced regularly so provide for yourself pillows for the floor, a blanket, a yoga mat, a candle and possibly a speaker for soft music or guided meditation.

First Workshop Assignment

It's important with this exercise to completely let your imagination go and your creativity flow. Imagine yourself at 90 years old and having lived a dream life with a dream job.

Take a sheet of paper and a pen and write a letter to you of today from you of the future. Describe everything you have accomplished in your personal life and work, how these accomplishments make you feel, and what you are most proud of.

Describe in the letter where you have lived, the most adventurous experience you had, the love in your life, and the deep gratitude and satisfaction that you feel for a life well lived.

This letter should be fun and inspiring. Don't think about how you will accomplish the things you write about. Dream big – so big that you can't imagine how you could possibly do these things.

Debbi Sluys, owner of Dare 2 Declare Academy, once told me that a goal is something you know you can accomplish already and how to get that done. A vision is a dream that you have no idea how to accomplish. You don't have to know the "how" and you have to accept that for this to work.

This isn't a planning session. It's a dreaming session. Have fun with it.

GRATITUDE PRACTICE

"Some people are always grumbling because roses have thorns; I am thankful that thorns have roses."

—Alphonse Karr

"Self love is an ocean
and your heart is a
vessel. Make it full, and
any excess will spill
over into the lives of
the people you hold
dear. But you must
come first."

—Beau Taplin

2

Swipe Right for Yourself

This workbook is for people feeling stuck.

I'm writing this for all of you who are divorced, never married, lost a partner or feel lost within your own life, your relationship or marriage and you are in search of a new way of life.

I'm a woman who took time to meet the new me after I was divorced, and a mission bloomed within me to help others do the same. I am still learning and know now that I want to always be learning, always be open to what life can show me.

First things first though. Let's talk about you and just how powerful you are.

You may not feel it right now, but I know this to be true. Meditation, therapy, travel, prayer, support groups and exercise are just a few ways you can begin to heal. For me, it was hiking and talking issues through with friends who will be honest with me and yet not try to fix me.

You have the power to heal yourself utilizing all these methods. You choose what works for you, but the trick is — you must choose. Therefore, the real power remains within you, within your choices. The power to heal always has been within you and it still is.

EMPOWERMENT PRACTICE 2: SEE YOURSELF GROWING

Visualization is a practice which requires repetition. Each week you will get a new visualization meditation. If it works for Olympic athletes, it can work for you. It's a small, practical thing that will provide a safe place for your heart and mind.

I have provided a recording for you in our syllabus website, but you can also record this for yourself on your smart phone and listen to it in the car, on your walks, in bed before you go to sleep.

Let's define a practice we will use in every chapter. It is called the Breathwork Five and goes like this.

Breathwork Five Practice

Take five deep breaths.

Count to five as you breath in, hold for three seconds,

Slowly release your breath counting to five as you breath out.

Clear your mind and picture the breath coming in and out of your lungs.

When you reach a state of relaxation, begin the recording.

MEDITATION

The time has come. Your seed is ready to transform into a beautiful, glorious flower.

Winter is over and the day grows longer. More sun comes each day to warm the earth.

The miracle of life and rebirth stand ready.

As the light of the sun warms the earth, your shell begins to slowly crack open. A small fragile stem peaks out, searching for the light.

Each day, the stem will grow and become stronger and stronger. The tender green shoot reaches for the warm earth, the life-giving light.

Then a miracle happens – the plant forms life-giving roots which grow deeper and stronger.

Days go by and a complex, fragile bud begins to form. It opens ever so slowly.

The petals release one at a time like tiny little fingers and reach for the light. The flower absorbs the light – reaching higher and higher each moment of the day.

The flower rests deeply and soundly at night. While the flower rests, the stems, the petals, the roots and the very core of the flower utilize the power of the light to grow and flourish.

The beauty and resources of the flower begin to bring joy and life to other beings – bees, birds, humans.

Within the flower, new life begins to form. New seeds are formed within this beautiful flower.

These seeds will bring life-sustaining joy and happiness to the world as you release them.

The process is eternal, the pattern of growth and giving and re-birth.

You have it within you to continue to grow. You are a bringer of light, joy and happiness.

Reach, reach, reach.

Repeat this meditation on a daily basis or substitute other guided meditations.

"Faith is taking the first
step even when you
don't see the whole
staircase."

—Martin Luther King, Jr.

3

What Do You Want for Yourself

"What are you hoping for in your new life?" Brandi asked me as we walked along the path together in 2018. We met while walking along the Camino de Santiago path in Spain.

You know those moments where you just go blank? Well, that was me. I knew what I *didn't* want more than I knew what I did.

She asked if I had ever made a vision board. I had not, but I'd seen them and heard of them. I had never tried it before.

She shared with me how she had started making vision boards several years back. She included her personal goals, work goals and family goals and she shared examples. The process was placing photos, text and clippings on a board/poster that would spark the vision for that year.

But here I was on a trail with a 20-pound backpack and no cork board.

"Well, I guess I'll do that when I get home," I said.

"Take out your phone and open your notes app," she says. "Let's talk for a few minutes about what you *DO* want in your life. What makes you happy? Write down a few words about your future," she said.

So, I started a list of what makes me happy:

- Dancing
- Traveling
- Running in a new city
- Meeting people
- Physical exertion
- Exercise challenges
- Kiss behind my ear
- Hugs from behind
- Long, slow dinner with friends
- Holding hands
- Morning sex
- Long slow kisses
- Kisses down my spine
- Sharing books

Then goals started to emerge:

- Traveling with my daughters
- Dating a dog lover
- Hiking with my partner
- Amount of $ when I sell my business
- Financial security post-sale
- Secure in love with no doubts

- Employment that brings travel and growth
- Live by the ocean

Over the duration of the seven-week Camino, this list became a place I could turn to and remind myself what made me feel good. I discussed the list with others and added to it along the way.

I had felt physically alone for a long time and when I started writing down these physical pleasures that I envisioned for myself, it became easier to feel it again. I hardly remembered how much I loved these things and how much of a physical creature I am. The seed was re-planted for me.

As I wrote further about how much money I wanted if I were to sell my business, I began to see my life without the day-to-day of the business. I was able to see past the sadness of giving up something I built. And it turned out, I DID get what I wrote down and I believe that early statement of what it was worth made a difference in how I approached the sale.

DID I MANIFEST IT? DID PRAYING WORK? I BELIEVE SO.

I am purposefully simplifying this process just so you have an example. It doesn't have to be intimidating or difficult. You don't have to take photos or cut pictures out of a magazine. You can just start with a list of words.

When I was around four years into the process of healing, I wanted some accountability for my new life on sabbatical. I began working with a life coach and she asked me to create a new vision board for myself. However, she had a new twist.

"Since you are a writer, why don't you write your own future story," she said. "Write about your new life and how it feels to be there. Put some time parameters on the vision and be as specific as you can."

I absolutely dreaded the exercise, but I was so glad she gave me a deadline! For some reason, I was afraid to write down my dreams – even though it had worked for me before. I share this so you know that I understand it is hard for most people. So, if it is hard for you, you are not alone.

Once I got started though, I couldn't stop. I could have been writing a freaking romance novel! This showed me where my heart was focusing.

I loved how my life looked in the future. I was inspired by the kindness, gratitude and love I could see in my future. My heart, like the Grinch, grew 10 times in size that day. I felt the positivity of the vision surrounding me, holding me gently and the wind in my face as I sailed into that future.

EMPOWERMENT PRACTICE 3: ENVISION YOUR BEST LIFE

Creating a vision board is not a cut-and-dry system. You must follow where your heart leads. What is the lowest "barrier to entry" for you?

Is your heart leading you to primarily use words, similar to my initial notes app brain dump? Use outline form if that is what feels good.

Are you a visual person and pictures most appeal to you? Use a poster board collage with images that inspire you or choose a digital vision board application.

Choose your method of vision board and give yourself a deadline for a completed first draft. This deadline should be just a few days because you have other projects ahead. This does not have to be perfect. This is the beginning of a process!

Focus your board on multiple aspects of your life, such as healthy habits, relationships, travel, finances and career.

The next few pages, we will get you started. Just follow the instructions and then run with it.

First use the Breathwork Five practice. Then keep your eyes closed and picture yourself in the new life.

Let's go!

Preparation

Picture yourself somewhere that makes you happy or where you believe you could be happy in the future. Is it a faraway place abroad? Is it Montana? Alaska? Italy?

List ten places where you would like to visit or even live.

1.
2.
3.
4.
5.
6.
7.
8.
9.
10.

Relationships are where we can feel most loved and joyful when you choose wisely who you spend your time with. List people in your life already and people you want to meet. If you seek a relationship, give this person a pseudonym.

List ten people you want to spend time with over the next year.

1.
2.
3.
4.
5.
6.
7.
8.
9.
10.

Let's keep going. Now picture yourself doing things. Is it running, hiking, shopping, sailing, or walking on a beach?

List ten action words or verbs that make you smile.

1.
2.
3.
4.
5.
6.
7.
8.
9.
10.

Being healthy and feeling full of energy just makes everything in your life better. Be as ambitious as you want and keep in mind exercise can be done just about anywhere in the world!

List ten things you will do to improve and maintain your health.

1.
2.
3.
4.
5.
6.
7.
8.
9.
10.

Now is when it gets fun!

Let's Get Curious

Examine both the letter from your workshop exercise and this exercise. List all these keywords that were weaved into both. These words are clues from your subconscious and are there to provide guidance.

Meditate

Take time now to do the Breathwork Five preparing for a short meditation. This meditation will be different because you will be opening your eyes.

Have the list of words in front of you where you are meditating. You will focus on one word at a time seeking inspiration from your subconscious and your imagination.

Read the word, close your eyes and slowly repeat the word several times. Allow pictures to come to your mind's eye to show you what the word can mean. Ask your subconscious to show you why this word is important in your life.

Vision Board

How will feel most creative while making your vision board? Is that photography? Is it creating a digital vision board, a physical poster board, or do you want to write a story of your future? You decide and I'm here to help if you wish to discuss in our Facebook Group.

Gather your materials in your workshop and allow the creativity to flow. Check our workbook website for links to online resources for digital vision boards.

Share

When you feel you have a good first draft, share it with someone you trust. Don't "sell" them on your vision board. Ask them what they see and listen. Just listen.

Sit with the project and the feedback for two days and then revisit the project. Likely, you will have some revisions or additions as you have thought about it throughout the week.

Make it a practice to revisit the vision board monthly and assess what's happening. I believe you will be delighted how your vision comes to life.

GRATITUDE FOCUS

"It is not joy that makes us grateful; it is gratitude that makes us joyful."

—David Steindl-Rast

“You are enough.
You are so enough.
It is unbelievable
how enough you
are.”

—Sierra Boggess

4

You Are Enough

When I finally admitted to myself that my marriage was over, one of the first people I told was my sister-in-law, Carrie. Telling people so close to both of us was going to be a huge step for me because I knew it was something I wouldn't be able to take back. Carrie was aghast, sorrowful and supportive. She did all she could do — listen.

After telling Carrie, I headed home to get cleaned up. The challenge of getting ready for work every day was exhausting. I loved my work, but I didn't want to go through the motions. I wanted to crawl in bed and cry — which, of course, was the worst thing for me.

I made it to the office and tried to focus on the company. Shortly after, Carrie walked in. She shut my office door and sat down with me. She handed me a gift and asked me to open it.

The gift was two bracelets.

One said, "I am enough" and the second said "My story is not over."

I was so touched and immediately put them on. These bracelets reminded me every day, all day, that I was loved. And many people stopped me after seeing the bracelet "I am enough" and shared that it touched them to see those words. Some even told me their own story.

This week you will focus on seeing yourself as more than enough. You are going to put to practice the act of loving yourself.

My friend Faith once said to me, "So be grateful for those hard moments because they've made you who you are. And when you figure out that you are enough — and that you're not just enough — you're pretty great. It's all worth it."

EMPOWERMENT PRACTICE 4: LIFE PURPOSE RESUME

This chapter is all about your worth and how you value yourself. Some of us have been at-home moms. Some have had amazing careers. Some of us have lived a sweet, small-town life that was everything we had dreamed of. Many of us however have had hardship. And some of us are hurting like hell right now. I've been there.

But we have ALL accomplished things in our lives. Accomplishments don't make us who we are, and they are not our purpose. Your purpose is the impact you want to make on the world.

We have probably all had to build a resume at some point, and we list all of our work accomplishments. But what about what you are called to do — then and now? Look back at your non-work life, you will see how your past actions can show you your purpose.

By visiting your memories of what brought you joy, you will see where you made an impact, and you will remember that feeling. I want you to dive deep, so you find that feeling again.

Let's get started!

Using the insight you have gained from your workshop letter and your vision board, you will now create a Life Purpose Resume. This is building toward a defined life purpose statement. Use this time to go deep within to remember the times in your life that you felt most whole, accomplished and seen.

Read through these instructions completely before you begin the exercise pages.

1. Practice the Breathwork Five and prepare yourself to begin. Picture yourself in your happiest moment as you breath.

2. Write one sentence about what you want for yourself. For example, *With all I have learned in my life, I am going to be an amazing non-profit leader, a faithful and kind partner and the best grandma ever seen.*

3. Write down your deeply personal accomplishments in the pages provided. List what makes you happy when you reminisce. This isn't about business. This is about emotions and love. For example:

    - I raised three incredibly talented, empathetic, loving and fun daughters.

    - I built a loving household where my friends and family felt welcome.

    - I entertained and put a smile on many people's faces.

    - I served on non-profit boards and made a difference in the community.

4. Now list 3 things you loved about the experience especially about how it made you feel. Keep it simple. If it makes you smile, write it down. For example,

- I helped the child advocacy center raise money to help abused children.

- I gathered silent auction items for the fundraiser for the youth choir summer tour.

5. Now list 3 ways this experience affected your life and how it may have changed how you saw yourself. What did you do that you are proud of?

- Entertaining others fulfilled a need in me to serve others.
- Running marathons kept me healthy and better able to serve my family.

As you do this exercise, my hope is that you will see that all the little things you did in life add up to big things. They just might guide you to your future purpose.

Whatever has happened in your life that brought you to this book, nothing can take away all of the amazing things you have done in your life.

The smallest things: They are worthy of your remembrance.

May they bring you joy.

Let's begin!

In Search of My Life Purpose, I Make This Statement:

What I want for myself is...

Deeply Personal Accomplishment #1

3 things that I loved about this experience

1.

2.

3.

3 ways this affected my life and how I saw myself

1.

2.

3.

Deeply Personal Accomplishment #2

3 things that I loved about this experience

1.

2.

3.

3 ways this affected my life and how I saw myself

1.

2.

3.

Deeply Personal Accomplishment #3

3 things that I loved about this experience

1.

2.

3.

3 ways this affected my life and how I saw myself

1.

2.

3.

Deeply Personal Accomplishment #4

3 things that I loved about this experience

1.

2.

3.

3 ways this affected my life and how I saw myself

1.

2.

3.

Now that you have completed the resume layout. It's time to complete the first draft of your Life Purpose Statement.

You should be taking into account:

1. Your letter from Empowerment Practice 1.
2. Your visualization from Empowerment Practice 2
3. Your creative vision board from Empowerment Practice 3.
4. Your life purpose Resume from Empowerment Practice 4.

My Life Purpose

What brings me joy:

What I'm passionate about:

What I have to give:

My life purpose is to:

“You yourself, as
much as anybody in
the entire universe,
deserve your love and
affection.”

—Buddha

5

You Could Be Right.

At some point in everyone's life, there is a life-changing decision that must be made. When a crisis comes, that is usually a 'given' circumstance. The crisis may be born out of your own mistakes or other's choices. It may be born out of death or a different type of goodbye.

Situations that cause strife and are embedded in our subconscious and if not dealt with, can keep us from moving forward with our lives.

Something happened in your life that brought you to this workbook and the work you do here is going to improve your life. You are going to be happier, healthier, and see yourself in a whole new light.

But let's start with reframing this past situation. Can you look at your own part in the situation and take a step back. One way is to open your mind to the idea that the other person in the situation may, in some way, however small, have been justified or right in their beliefs. At the very least, you can acknowledge they did believe what they said.

The following practice is designed to help you let go of what is haunting you. Sharing your innermost pain and letting it dissolve into the ether. It can happen but it comes with time and practice.

EMPOWERMENT PRACTICE 5: REFRAME THE SITUATION

When we are in the heat of the battle, it can be difficult to see the core of the problem. When the pain is blinding, I daresay, it is near impossible.

What if we could let the pain or the situation sit beside us like an old friend? Just the thought of that is quite powerful to me.

Let's go a step further name the situation. Not death, divorce, infidelity, or failure.

Let's call it Friend or give it a name of someone who provides you comfort.

Friend is a peaceful presence, and it cannot hurt you. It is represented by a soft golden ball of light. You feel warm and safe in its presence. And because it does not have the power to hurt you, you can say anything to Friend.

In the following pages, you will record your reaction to the following exercise. Reflect on how you felt during the meditation and any trigger points that might have come up for you.

Read through the exercise. In the online syllabus, you will find an audio recording walking you through the meditation. Do not try to write as you do the exercise. Complete and then record your reflections.

Let's begin.

Close your eyes, in a quiet and safe place and practice the Breathwork Five. It is important that your mind is calm so you can welcome this conversation to your subconscious, your imagination.

When you are quiet and relaxed, say hello to Friend. Tell Friend about the situation that is bringing you pain and how this situation has affected your life.

Describe here how the situation makes you feel.

Now define for Friend the struggle you are facing. Your goal here is to name the core problem or challenge. Define both sides of the situation.

Now, it's time to turn the tables. Now you are the Friend.

Advise yourself as Friend on how to take the first step toward resolving the core problem. Could there be another way to view this?

What is the first step toward solution. Can you say, "You could be right"?

Now that you have named it and called it what it was, you are taking back your power. As long as the core problem was ruling your mind, the problem has your power.

You have just reclaimed your power. Congratulations! Be proud of yourself.

Now the next two steps are very important.

1. It is time to treat yourself. Do something kind and loving for yourself.

Once you do, list it here and then be grateful.

2. Now look yourself in the mirror and say,

Thank you for being brave.
Thank you for loving me enough to do the hard things.
You are going to be as happy as you have ever been.
Keep going.

GRATITUDE PRACTICE

"We often take for granted the very things that most deserve our gratitude."

—Cynthia Ozick

“To forgive is to set
a prisoner free and
discover that the
prisoner was you.”

—Lewis B. Smedes

6

Forgiveness Is Possible

I think many people have a hard time with the concept of forgiveness. I certainly have.

The challenge in forgiveness is that it isn't cut and dry and that it isn't something that you can do one time and it is over. Frequently the act of forgiveness is more like a daily routine such as taking a shower.

When there has been a betrayal, a loss of friendship, or the end of a relationship, many people, including me, get stuck in a place of pain. Even when you work through the pain and you begin to feel happy, you can be haunted by the circumstance or by the person who caused you the pain.

Pain has a boomerang effect that only you can halt. Until you can fully forgive who or what has hurt you, including yourself, the pain will be your unwanted constant companion.

It's time for you to embrace the freedom of forgiveness so that you can be set free.

In *The Art of Forgiving, When You Need to Forgive and Don't Know How* by Lewis Smedes, he provides three stages of forgiveness which really spoke to me. I will summarize these stages within the context of my own experience. I'm highlighting Smedes' stage in bold so you can recognize it as his definition.

STAGE ONE: "WE DISCOVER THE HUMANITY OF THE PERSON."

Many of us subconsciously fear that our forgiveness would excuse what the other person has done.

But forgiveness doesn't condone behavior, just like apologies don't erase the fact that it happened.

What you need to see now is this person's humanity as well as your own.

STAGE TWO: "SURRENDERING OUR RIGHT TO GET EVEN."

The way Smedes explains it, when in pain, we are reserving the right for vengeance, but we must learn that vengeance is certainly not going to give us happiness.

Being in a new or safe place and creating a new daily existence for yourself will make the necessity for vengeance melt away like snow.

Can you find a way to look at every situation that involves the other person with a loving eye. Can you look at every situation through the lens of love?

Vengeance is not only unhealthy but could potentially devastate you further. And more importantly, to seek vengeance could possibly harm your family and friends further.

It is hard to swallow. There are going to be no repercussions for the acts of betrayal that occurred. What is done is done.

You must let the fantasy of vengeance slip through your fingers like water and fall away where it will remain forever.

STAGE THREE: "REVISING OUR FEELINGS."

Smedes says that when we give up our right to get even and we see the offender's humanity, our feelings will change. Where before we felt hate, whether it be passive or aggressive, it can be replaced with forgiveness.

It can be hard for you to conceive of wishing happiness when someone has hurt you.

When I was introduced to the book *The Secret*, it gave me the words to use in my quest to forgive. I began to use those 12 words as a practice in hopes that not only could it be a true and lasting wish, but that it would bring me the peace and joy allowing me to move on with more finality.

These 12 powerful words. I forgive you. I release you. I want you to be happy.

I was reluctant to wish my ex-husband happiness because it meant he would be happy with the other person who had caused me so much pain.

Although I was reluctant and hesitant at first, once I began to find the benevolent intent behind my words, the more real it became.

In reality, I was also wishing for myself these same things.

It was me who needed to be released.

It was me that needed happiness.

And I held the key to unlock those things for myself.

This was my miracle. I could find a way to forgive, to release and to wish happiness for the two people who had hurt me most in my life.

This was Grace I was receiving. I was taking back my power and shining light into my own life. No matter how much my friends and family loved me, I had to do this for myself.

FORGIVE YOURSELF

Many people have asked me what was the greatest lesson I learned on the Camino. My answer has always been that I learned to forgive my ex-husband and more importantly, myself. I get some funny looks on the second part of that statement. I see the question in their eyes.

I had always been a strong person and someone that my friends and family could rely on. I was a joyful person and I loved to give. I could also be stubbornly focused on achieving a goal.

But when it came time to protect myself from the person I loved most, I failed. I failed to stand up for myself. I failed to recognize what was right in front of me. I didn't leave when I could see I was unloved. I didn't stay married like I had dreamed.

Writing this book has given more weight to the statement that I had to forgive myself. Just as I continually worked to forgive Garth and Miranda, I continued the work toward my own forgiveness.

So here, I say it again...

Kelly,

I forgive you.
I release you.
I wish you happiness.

You are loved.
You are more than enough.
The best is yet to come.

EMPOWERMENT PRACTICE 6:
MEDITATION 3 STEPS TO FORGIVENESS

Smedes' outline for the stages of forgiveness provided me a way to outline my process for you. Now I want to offer a meditation for you to use if you need to walk the pathway to forgiveness.

Forgiveness is so hard. It has taken me years. This is what worked for me, and it may be a variation of this that works for you. Please explore and add to the meditation if it helps you.

This practice involves seeing the wounds on both parties, not just yours. It's been hard for me to accept that the other party is also injured but it stands to be true.

Breathing is probably the most important part of this practice. Keeping yourself in a relaxed state will help you gain more insight as you walk toward peace.

Go to your workshop and prepare for this meditation. Let's go there now.

Practice your Breathwork Five. An audio file has been provided in the online course and you can hit play when you are ready to begin.

The Person

After you have reached a state of relaxation, continue to breathe normally. Consider who you might need to forgive by picturing them in your mind and mentally quietly saying their name.

It is certainly a valid practice to also consider the need to forgive yourself.

The point of this exercise is release. The most important step is to recognize that everyone is wounded, including the person you need to release.

Concentrate on where you feel the pain in your body when you think of this person. Is it your heart, your abdomen, your arm, your hips, your neck?

It may not be pain, but rather a simple sensation or awareness. Breathe into this part of your body. And take a deep breath again.

The Wound

In your mind's eye, visualize there is a wound on the person you want to forgive in that spot where you feel the pain.

With care, treat this same wounded area on the person you seek to forgive. You slowly roll a bandage over the wound and symbolically cover their sin or betrayal against you.

You are recognizing this person also has wounds within this relationship and you can both heal. If it is yourself you are seeking to forgive, apply the bandage over your body where you feel the pain.

The bandage is symbolic of empathy, release and forgiveness. Breathe deeply.

1. Next, look at the betrayal and the offending party as if through an unfocused lens of a camera. It is hazy and unclear. As you turn the dial, you create a different perspective.

Now this lens is clearly in focus and is seen from the perspective of a disinterested party who does not feel the need for vengeance or payback. This person can only see the humanity in the mistakes that were made during the betrayal.

Can you be this person looking through the lens?
Can you look through the lens with an objective view?
Can you look at the situation with detachment?
Can you begin to see through a new lens of forgiveness?

This doesn't have to be complete, total or final — just a start.

2. Next, can you put words to how you feel after seeing their humanity through a new lens and through the healing bandage? Can you maintain a relaxed state in your mind and body?

   Can you repeat these words?

   I forgive you.
   I release you.
   I wish you happiness.

   And to yourself, say these words.

   I release myself from the pain of your betrayal.
   I release myself from the need for payback.
   I release myself from this sense of un-belonging.

3. Lastly, you're going to state your intention for happiness. You don't have to use my words, but they are there as a guide. Deep down you know what you need and deep down you know what you want.

   I seek peace at all times.
   I seek joy at all times.
   I live in a state of happiness.
   I shine my light on others in love.
   I bring empathy and kindness to others.

Lay down for 10 to 15 minutes after this exercise. Keep your mind quiet but try to absorb those last statements of intention. If your mind begins to wander, come back to the intention. This is something you can do every day.

GRATITUDE PRACTICE

"Acknowledging the good that you already have in your life is the foundation for all abundance."

—Eckhart Tolle

“Out of your vulnerabilities will come your strength.”

—Sigmund Freud

7

Courage Redefined

These steps back into reality take courage and courage is now going to be re-defined for you. Courage is going to have a whole new look. Your new courage is not quite like an athlete who crosses the finish line. It's a bit like a boxer fighting in the ring. But there is a path for you to follow.

The type of courage you need now starts with vulnerability. But I can hear you now — "*WTF? How could I be any more vulnerable?*"

Brené Brown's *Call to Courage* on Netflix has changed a lot of people's minds about vulnerability, and it also gives a great deal of insight into shame and guilt.

After watching the video, even though I was alone in my house, I began to say aloud things I had felt while watching. Brown's words lit a spark in me. I instantly recognized some non-negotiables deep within my soul and I said them out loud. The sound of my voice was convincing, and it felt good to fill the room with the sound of my hope.

I will not close myself off from the possibility of love.
I will not close myself off to moving on.
I will not be afraid to find out what the "new me" is going to do in my life.
And I will not stop believing in love.

Then, I realized these were spoken in a negative frame of mind, almost like I was giving myself new limitations, when using the words "I will not." So, I started over with "I can" and began lifting myself up with statements of belief in myself.

I can get up and go for a walk every day and I'll bring a friend if I need the support.
I can begin to look at job listings to find out what interests me.
I can listen to music that builds me up.
I can start a list of what I like about myself.
I can begin to look in the mirror every day and say I love you to myself.
I can go buy myself a new dress, negligee or underwear — something that makes me feel pretty.
I can see that all of my accomplishments still matter.
I can feel I'm loved and admired by my children.
I can believe I will be loved deeply again someday.
I can, I can, I can, and I will.

What are your limiting beliefs? Do you feel worthy of what you have established as your vision and your purpose in the previous exercises. Be courageous and examine how you feel about your deservingness and let's do the exercise.

EMPOWERMENT PRACTICE 7: LET'S GET VULNERABLE

"Courage is the willingness to show up when you can't control the outcome," shares Brown in her Netflix special.

Your homework is to watch the *Call to Courage* or Brown's Ted Talk on YouTube which is free. After you watch the video, consider how you are currently living your life. You are successful and strong, and I know this because you are doing this work.

Do you have the opportunity to be vulnerable on a daily basis or are you busy being the superhero, the boss, and/or the mom?

It's time to take a step back from your daily life and your daily responsibilities. The priority in your life must be you and the reason that is going to resonate with you is that a better you is going to bring more to the world around you.

If you stay stuck, the world is missing out. You must choose you and when you do, everyone around you will know that their world is a better place. Your renewed energy will redefine how you relate to others and how you give back to the world.

Are you ready? I believe you are.

The next exercise is a chance to woman-up and I know it may be hard to see it. But I've been there, and I believe you can do it.

Let's go girl!

Instructions:

Write down 10 ways you can be courageous through vulnerability. Think through who you want to be — not who you have been. You are declaring action steps to get you to your vision and discovering how to embody your life purpose.

What actions can you take that propel you into the future? **For example, here are some prompts:**

1. I can show up and be seen by...

2. I can ask for what I need by...

3. I can talk about how I'm feeling with...

4. I can have a hard conversation with...

5. I can look at myself in the mirror and say...

6. Your turn...

7. Again...

8. Next...

9. Again...

10. Last but not least...

Keep the list going and see all the ways you can show up for yourself.
Then, take it one step further...
Pick one that you will follow through with this week.

This week I will show up for myself by...

Pick another that you will follow through two weeks from now.

Within two weeks, I will show up for myself by...

I encourage you to put a date by EVERY courageous and vulnerable action.

GRATITUDE PRACTICE

"I don't have to chase extraordinary moments to find happiness – it's right in front of me if I'm paying attention and practicing gratitude."

—Brené Brown

“The real art of con-
versation is not only
to say the right thing
at the right place but
to leave unsaid the
wrong thing at the
tempting moment.”

—Dorothy Nevill

8

The Words in Your Head and Heart

NO person has ever been or will ever be in your situation.

This is an intensely personal moment/day/week/year. Your life, your feelings and your past are uniquely your own. Only you know what is actually going on inside your head and heart.

Therefore, I will repeat — you have the power to heal yourself.

When you have had a significant event in your life, people often don't know what to say to you. We all know that empty feeling of wanting to comfort someone who lost a loved one and we believe no words can possibly comfort them. Actually, much healing can come from words in a time of need, as well as a tender touch, a hug, holding a hand, or just simply sitting with someone in silence.

You can start today. You can start tomorrow. You can start next year. But you will eventually have to make decisions about next steps and those will lead to your new life.

I want to share with you a conversation between me and my friend Alison. The was originally published in my book.

Kelly

What is a good piece of advice that you received from someone, anyone that made a difference in your life when you were going through a big change?

Alison

There are many, many, many, but the one that I really recall again and again and again,

...my best friend said to me,
"This is going to look different in a year."

Then she would even whittle it down to "this will look different next week."

It actually put things more in perspective. When I felt really stuck and entangled and "this is what it's going to be forever" feeling, I knew that it's not going to last, it's temporary and that it will shift and that if I just don't focus on my belief that it's permanent, then I can recognize that it is temporary and just relax into the knowing that it's gonna change.

Kelly

That's pretty similar to what you asked me that day (in 2021). You were leading me in a totally different way, and I want to talk about that.

Do you remember clearly what you said when we were in the room? You were leading me down the path to think differently about my past or how it would feel. Could I get to a place where I felt differently about it?

Alison

I seem to recall, it was something along the lines of, "Have you considered the possibility of that?" Because we had talked about the fact that [your ex-husband's relationship with] Miranda was a substantial relationship?

It was obviously substance, she was a substantial person in his life, because they had been together at this point for 12 years. And the realization of that — it wasn't a fling; it was another substantial person. And the consideration that this doesn't take away from your value in his life. That was one part of it.

Because you're obviously a very substantial person in his life. And then the second part, "Have you considered the possibility that he went into a relationship with her because you needed to go out into your life and do something else?"

And it wasn't about him leaving you, but setting you free, even if it was unconscious.

Kelly

You were presenting it to me in a way that even in that moment, I didn't get it. It was a couple of months later, when I was listening to The Secret [by Rhonda Byrne], and the writer was saying that if we're feeling pain, it is because we're manifesting pain, or we're holding on to pain from something in the past.

And as long as you're hanging on to that pain, you're gonna keep feeling it. I kept saying I've let it go. I kept saying and I kept believing that I had let it go. And maybe I did. But then I kept pulling it back.

That theme of rejection. I've really been working on that.

When you gave that advice, was it coming from a place that somebody had said it to you? Or had shown you that lesson?

Or was it just something, in the moment, that you saw in me that made you share it?

Alison

I feel like that it wasn't something that someone had said to me, but it was a realization that I had about my own life. I guess it was with my marriage, maybe. But it showed up later, a few years later in another relationship.

And the recognition that life is happening for me, not to me, and that I'm the starring attraction in my life.

How do I want myself to be even in those moments of terror and tragedy and devastation?

We still are totally free to choose how we want to be and how we want to show up and how we respond. I feel like some of that knowledge came along the path of the yogic teachings that I've received over the past three decades and also through the realization and the experience that comes by being immersed in those teachings.

For me, that's been my pathway. And what I heard you say is that you've received it through walking the Camino, you've received it through being inquisitive and curious in relationships with other people as well as through the program that you said you were in [Calling in "The One"] during the summer and reading some books that were beneficial to you. That helped to flesh out some of those pieces.

It's really the same mountain. It's just different pathways. And the pinnacle at the top of the mountain is the recognition that we are free, and we've always been free, and we will always be free.

Alison

One of the most profound lessons that I learned was that in the past I had this belief about myself that I wasn't good enough. And I chose the perfect weather pattern and storm and partner and container and life to reflect that for me so that I could learn that lesson.

That was my belief and then also I had to unpack it so that I could be free of that belief.

Kelly

Yeah. Wow.

Alison

I would see it everywhere and it would show up everywhere. But the closest relationship was the one that really highlighted it for me so dramatically that I couldn't not see it and couldn't not attend to it.

Because I'm a self-curious person, I stayed with it. You know, I did. I constantly do the work. And I know not everybody is like that, but I'm grateful that I am. Because it encourages me to just keep expanding.

Kelly

I felt like I kept along those same lines.

I was doing Bible studies and I was doing everything I could to learn to be a good person without ever addressing my own stuff. I think something's going to come out of that. I don't know how this all ends up in the book or what that looks like, but I think that so many women do this. We grow up doing exactly what we were told we should do. We want to be a good person. Do all the right things.

Alison

I feel like those things are externally focused. And that's where the disconnect happens.

There's a separation so that if I put all my attention in the external or outside world, I'm going to feel whole. I'm going to feel complete.

But it's not out there, it's actually within us. All of our perceptions are based on our beliefs and how we're looking [at it], what color glasses we're wearing.

Basically, what is the lens that we're looking through?

It wouldn't really matter what changed on the outside because the lens is the same. We have to look at the lens and tend to that.

So, it's an introversion — an introverted experience. And within that, when we return to the scriptures, like when we read the Bible, we can see more clearly what it's actually pointing to. And again, it's pointing back to you the truth that you are divine, because you have been created in the image of God. You are God. God is all around us and within us.

Kelly

Therefore, you can affect your own universe. You have to stop feeling helpless and stop thinking you can't do anything about this. Exactly. You have all the power to do it — you have the power.

Alison

You <u>are</u> power. Yeah.

Kelly

I know we can't control if a car hits our car.

When you hear something, when somebody shares something with you, honor that it was shared with you and hold it. Just hold it inside, maybe in a secret place, until you're ready to deal with it.

Or if somebody's noticing something about you then just accept it. It can be a year later; it can be five years later.

When somebody says something to you, don't dismiss it, because it might find a place in your healing going forward.

Alison

We're always right where we're meant to be. I mean, all these lessons to get right here right now. Right?

Kelly

Yeah. And the last question is: Any last advice for people who are going through a big change?

Alison

Yeah, just be patient and gentle with yourself. And just love yourself. Nourish yourself. Be kind and loving to yourself.

What do we want from others?
We have to give it to ourselves first.

Yeah, the most important equation in the whole room.

Kelly

Yeah. How do you treat yourself?

Alison

That's the most important piece. Be kind and gentle.

EMPOWERMENT PRACTICE 8: THIS WILL LOOK DIFFERENT NEXT WEEK

As we heard from Alison, her best friend gave her a piece of advice that continually helps her reframe a situation.

Her best friend said to her, "This is going to look different in a year."

Then she would even whittle it down to "This will look different next week."

It actually put things more in perspective for Alison and she was able to let go of the feeling that her pain, frustration or anger would be a permanent fixture in her life.

And then Alison asked me, "Have you considered the possibility that he went into a relationship with her because you needed to go out into your life and do something else?"

That absolutely reframed my pain as an opportunity. I was quite sure I would not have sold the company, would not hiked two Caminos and I wouldn't be this strong woman I am now.

Your exercise for this chapter is to reframe a situation that has you stuck. What is going on in your life that is constantly on your mind?

Get out a pen and paper or open a blank document on your computer.

Prepare by doing the Breathwork Five and then begin.

1. Write down a list of the situations that have you stuck and the related emotions, whether that is pain, anger, humiliation, grief, abandonment or any other tough emotion.

2. Now, think to yourself, "This is going to look different next year." In fact, it is going to look different next week and maybe even today.

3. Let's pretend we are sitting together. How could I reframe your situation with a question? "Have you considered the possibility that....?"

   Write down your question. Really push yourself here. No one will know but you.

4. Now meditate on the question. Try to be still and repeat the question to yourself. Set a timer if you need to for five minutes or even more if you need that time.

5. Now attempt to answer the question. How can you reframe what this will look like next week and then next year?

This exercise is something I did many times. It took months for me to reframe my situation to my satisfaction but each time I did, it became easier, and I felt more peace. I hope you will too.

GRATITUDE PRACTICE

"We can only be said to be alive in those moments when our hearts are conscious of our treasures."

—Thornton Wilder

“There is a seed
planted in loss that
contains the horizon
you are longing for.”

—Toko-pa Turner

9

Grief and Loss: Permanently Temporary

Grief is defined in *On Grief and Grieving* by two authors Elisabeth Kübler-Ross and David Kessler as having five stages: denial, anger, bargaining, depression and acceptance. They later added a sixth stage called finding meaning.

My personal experiences with grief vary from loss of a sister-in-law to loss of a best friend. I am sure your personal experiences vary widely as well. I'd like to tell you a little bit about loss in my life. I lost all my grandparents at such a young age; I was too young to process it. It was in my thirties that I first faced death.

I lost a loved family member in 1998 to cancer. The family member fought bravely for five years, and we were grateful for the time we had with her. It would never be enough, but we were able to say our goodbyes. Having this opportunity lends itself to a different way of processing grief. Of course, this first major loss also taught me that time is not promised and about living in gratitude.

In 2008, another family member of mine experienced a traumatic accident that left them needing permanent care at the age of 50 and although they survived, it was an extremely difficult time for our family. We were so grateful he survived, and our family pulled together to help him achieve his greatest possible independence, but it was also a time of deep grief and trauma in many lasting ways.

We all handle grief differently. I always thought I could handle crises well — make a plan and go forward. Taking action and rallying around people who need me has never been hard for me. My understanding of who I was in a crisis had always been the same, until I experienced the loss of my marriage. Then I froze. It was definitely the deepest grief I've ever felt up to that point. You have been reading about the processing of this grief throughout this book.

Then, in 2022, when I lost one of my lifelong friends, Dan, it was quite a shock. He was healthy and happy and living his dream of sailing Mexico in the winter. I joined his crew in November 2021 to compete in a sailing rally from San Diego to Mexico. As a first-time team, we came in second place in our division — I do have to brag for Dan.

During the 30-day sailing rally, we had a lot of time to reminisce but also to dream of the future. He encouraged me to write and tell the stories I had swimming around in my head and heart. I feel so blessed that I had that experience with him before he died.

His accident and death came right as I was embarking on my second Camino in Portugal. It was a tough way to grieve because I was alone and far away. But Dan was the one who encouraged me to walk my first Camino to heal from my divorce. Therefore, it was quite poignant that I was on the trail while grieving him. I felt him with me every day.

Coming home from that Camino, I felt a change in my grieving process. It wasn't about taking action anymore.

It was about letting the pain come to me on the trail, letting the tears wash away the sadness, and letting my laughter be the light and love I had for my friend.

I talked to him throughout and still talk to him almost every day. I can hear him answer, "You're doing great, Kel."

With this chapter, I want to acknowledge the important part that the grief process plays in our lives. There is no right or wrong way to do it. And there is relief and healing when we share the grief with others. *Grief is like water; the more you spread it around, the faster it evaporates.*

You just have to be IN IT.

You must walk THROUGH IT.

And then you must ACCEPT AND LET IT GO as best you can.

Timing is everything and grief is one of those challenges in life that has its own timeline. You move from one stage to another, but not in a straight line and you can go back and forth, forwards and backwards.

My friend Kaye shared with me, "Grief is like fingerprints — no two are alike, so trust where you are, claim it, and keep going."

I believe if you are reading this book, you are likely in one of the stages of grief, even if you don't necessarily have an obvious loss to point to. The loss that initiates grief is not always physical.

We can experience loss through death, but there is an infinite list of ways we can feel loss — loss of friendship, loss of physical capabilities, loss of a previous way of life or financial security, change in your health or a loved one's health, aging, losing a job or opportunity.

Let's identify and work through the grief in your life.

EMPOWERMENT PRACTICE 9: HEALING IN LETTER WRITING

Many people use letter writing to express emotions. Sometimes that is a love letter, a Dear John letter and sometimes it is a way to relieve grief or pain.

I've been advised several times in my life to write a letter as a way of moving through a situation. I taught my children to use this powerful exercise and I believe it helped them at a young age learn to express emotions and find their words.

When I was grieving the loss of my marriage, I was advised by my life coach to write a letter to the woman my husband was involved with. Upon re-reading that letter, I saw a feeling of powerlessness in my words.

The perceived lack of control in the situation was haunting me and I had not seen that on my own until I wrote that letter. I was able to address that with the second letter of this exercise.

Remember, this is for you. No one needs to see this but you. Reading your own words is a powerful tool for recovery because you can identify the core of your needs.

You have space provided to write your letter here by hand.

Get to your safe and quiet workshop. Do what you need to do to feel safe. Is that a blanket wrapped around you? Is that making a nest in your bed?

Let's begin.

To Whom It May Concern

Write a letter to express your grief. Address your feelings of loss. That may be for a friend, a parent, a child, a spouse or a partner dear to you.

You have two pages to write your letter:

Letter continues:

Create Your Mantra

Once you have written the letter, create a phrase that makes sense for coping with/helping with this situation and we will use it in your meditation. For example,

- "All will be well"
- "I can move through this"
- "The best is yet to come"
- "I take back my power"
- "I am beloved"
- "I release this pain"

Write your mantra here:

Let It Flow

Now set a timer and meditate for 10 minutes. Imagine the grief as warm water in a pitcher being poured slowly over your head. It runs from the tip of your head, slowly down your face, your shoulders, your torso, your legs and your feet.

Be kind and loving to yourself in this space and allow the grief to flow through and over you. As you meditate, the grief washes over you and flows away. As it flows away, it evaporates.

This is a practice you can use on a regular basis when grief becomes overwhelming.

Grief is like water; the more you spread it around, the faster it evaporates.

Right Back Atcha

After your meditation, write a second letter. This letter is from the person you've lost, and it's written to you. This person is sharing how they feel about you and then they will share five things he/she loves about you.

If it helps, think of the happiest moment with this person or a time before the loss. Write from this point of view about that moment. This person is writing to you about their love and gratitude for you.

Write your letter here:

Five Things I Love About You

Possible prompts include:

- I love it when you...
- You always made me laugh when you...
- What I admire most about you...
- I always knew you cared when you...

1.

2.

3.

4.

5.

GRATITUDE PRACTICE

"There is always, always, always something to be thankful for."

—Unknown

“Wherever I go, there
are my people,”

says my friend Crystal.

10

Community: Find Your People

The older you become, the more aware you become that everyone is going through something. Everyone faces loneliness — especially when starting over and starting to date. Throw in an added layer of not having dated since you were in your twenties and the challenges seem more daunting.

Dating in its very base form is full of vulnerability. You are destined to receive rejection as well as having to reject a suitor.

This is why it is important to be in community with other like-minded individuals.

Being welcomed and being accepted by friends, new and old, is a vital part of recovering from big changes in life.

In the beginning, it can be important simply as a physical presence. Later, as friendships develop or deepen, the people around you can provide feedback, an honest assessment of the situation and a source of wisdom outside your own heart and mind.

SEEKING JOY

I recently read *The Book of Joy: Lasting Happiness in a Changing World* by the Dalai Lama, Desmond Tutu and narrated by Douglas Abrams. The book is a conversation where two world leaders come together to discuss the most important topic of joy.

This is where I first learned of the concept of Ubuntu, an African way of life, which means to have interdependence on each other.

"A person is a person through another person," said Tutu in *The Book of Joy*.

Tutu shares that we don't exist without two people coming together as parents. We don't learn to talk or walk without other humans.

"We belong in a delicate network. It is actually quite profound," said Tutu.

He goes on to explain that the village residents believe this so deeply that their greeting is "How are we?" instead of the Western greeting of "How are you?"

Also in this book, the Dalai Lama shared the lesson of Mudita, the concept of sympathetic joy. It is one of the Four Immeasurables of Buddhism which also include loving-kindness, compassion and equanimity.

Jinpa, the translator in the book, explains that.

"Mudita recognizes that life is not a zero-sum game, that there is not just one slice of cake in which someone else's taking more means we get less. Mudita sees joy as limitless."

For me these two concepts tie together the community that supports and uplifts a person in need.

Can we feel so connected that we understand that how you feel affects me?

Can we connect on a level where I am always happy for you and your success, your love and your wealth as if it were my own?

If we feel this connection and this lack of envy, there is a natural outgrowth of compassion.

EMPOWERMENT PRACTICE 10: FIVE WAYS TO GET OUT IN THE WORLD

This exercise is about stepping out of your box and stretching your wings.

When I separated from my husband, I needed to move. I had decided to hike the Camino at that point, so I joined some hiking groups on Meetup. This is a local app where interest groups can connect. Even still, hiking and running were great, but they weren't enough.

The lonely quiet evenings were killer for me. So, I started exploring Meetups for things other than hiking. I saw dancing. OH. MY. GOSH. I love dancing and the thought of getting lost on the dance floor sounded perfect.

I put on my dancing shoes and went to free salsa dance lessons I found online. I figured, hey, I'm going to Spain. Why not learn to salsa?

So, I encourage you to lean on your existing community but also lean into a new challenge to meet new people and try new things. Stepping out of your comfort zone, your neighborhood, your gym, whatever... it will help you in a unique way. You will be proud of yourself — even if you can't salsa (because that was me).

The challenge is to browse, peruse and explore the thought of doing new things. And I challenge you to take one step more. Sign up for something new!

Social App Tools

Meetup is a connection website service that you can access online or in the app.

- Outdoor activity groups are easy to find.

- Foodie groups are fun!

- There are specific groups for men, women or co-ed such as Singles Over 50, Travel Adventures for Singles.

- Just search for what you are interested in, and you will find a group!

Take a Class

What you always wanted to learn but didn't? Want to try new computer skills?

- Sometimes organizations will host speakers about traveling.
- How about a craft class like painting or sewing?
- Local libraries have amazing classes, and some are free!

Volunteer

Volunteer in the community. Do something that makes you feel like you are giving back. Giving to others is one of the healthiest ways to heal yourself.

- Homeless shelters always need help or supplies.
- Local churches usually have outreach programs to serve underserved populations.
- Tutor underprivileged children.
- Volunteer at a Boys and Girls Club or a local YMCA after school program.
- You can volunteer to help with the book returns or shelving books.
- Volunteer at a local animal shelter. They need help with dog walking and supplies.
- Volunteer at a senior center providing your skills to help others.

Join An Organization

- Join a church or cultural club such as a book club or a wine tasting club.

- Join your local Rotary Club, Lions Club or Chamber of Commerce.

- Join a new gym or athletic club that interests you.

- Join a pickleball or another low-pressure team.

Be the Host

Start inviting people to do things together. Game nights, sporting events, trivia nights — anything works! Just do it.

The new you is out there and you are fabulous. Go get 'em!

GRATITUDE PRACTICE

"Love those who appreciate you and appreciate those who love you."

—Connor Chalfant

"Don't try to change people. Make a realistic decision about where they fit in your life based on who they are, not who you want them to be."

—tinybuddha.com

11

Believe Them the First Time

In a world where texting is the norm (over speaking) and sarcasm runs rampant, how are we supposed to decipher what is happening in a relationship? We read other meanings into words in a text, or we miss completely what someone is trying to say.

Kayce gave me some great advice one night.

I'd gone on a first date and the guy, Sam, told me he was an a**hole, he was broke and he was also a chauvinist. Well, I'd never had anyone say these words to me — most men deny it — so I thought he was joking. Go ahead — laugh. I DO!

The next day, I'm having a glass of wine with Kayce, and she shares a quote from Maya Angelou that says:

"When people show you who they are,
believe them the first time."

In all my naivete and just being used to family sarcasm, I chose to believe he was just being self-deprecating. He wasn't. He was all those things. I won't say I wasted my time because I learned valuable lessons, but...

Listen to Maya!

Another example. I met Blake on Bumble. He was in town for a wedding, and we decided to meet. We clicked on a fun level, an emotional level and a chemistry level, but we also had some similar tough experiences in our life that brought us close quickly.

We ended up having four dates in one weekend. This was so good for me in many ways because I was able to be completely open with him and he helped me feel like a desirable woman. But he did not want a long-distance relationship.

No matter how much fun we had, no matter how hot the chemistry was, he said no relationship, just keep it casual.

It took four times of going back before I could see it wasn't just that. He eventually shared with me other reasons why it wouldn't work for him. In our last encounter in 2022, I saw something new in him, something I had not seen before and that surprised me. What I learned surprised me and showed me that we weren't in fact the match I thought we were. Finally, I could let go. Again, I learned lessons, so no regrets.

Don't be afraid to make mistakes. It is how we learn.

I'm telling you about both of these encounters for example's sake, but of course, there was more nuance to every situation.

What is important is — <u>you learn each time you date someone</u>.

Maybe the lesson won't be clear at the moment of the breakup. Sometimes, fear, shame or doubt can come during pre-breakup and cloud your thinking. But you can always find a lesson to learn from.

What is also true is that if you don't put yourself out there, you might not learn, you might not grow and you might not find what you need.

It's hard to fail but it is harder to get to what you truly want without these lessons or without trying.

EMPOWERMENT PRACTICE 11: WHAT DO I NEED TO OWN

I've suggested in Chapter 2 that you create a resume, make a list of your qualities and to do this, you need to make time for reflection. But you also need to look at yourself within the relationships you have had. From parents to siblings, from dating to marriage, friendships to breakups, you need to look for repeated behavior.

Can you identify cycles in your own behavior? Remember my story about Sam? Let's pretend you are him for a minute. If you were going to warn someone on a first date about your bad traits or habits, what would they be?

Go for it. Write it down. No one has to see it unless you want. There might be some shame there and there might be some pride. Whatever you see, write it down.

YOU ARE HUMAN! You have made mistakes. We all do. Take a look at yourself deep within, see and name the repeated behaviors and then forgive yourself.

Start by answering these questions and see if they reveal repeated behaviors:

1. Within your nuclear family, as a child, how did you act out within your parental relationships?

   Example: I was constantly needing attention from my father.

2. If you have siblings, how did you interact within those relationships in the early years?

   Example: I was resentful of my older sister's overprotective nature.

3. While dating at a young age, what behaviors do you remember?

   Example: I tended to be very serious too quickly.

4. Within your early friendships, how did your relationships emerge and evolve?

   Example: I wanted to be friends with more popular people and was eager for their attention. I became a doormat.

5. Within a marriage or partnership, how did you handle conflict?

   Example: I never backed down in a fight and fully believed I was right.

Now, review all these patterns and try to define where you can take responsibility. This is when you begin to heal and begin to forgive yourself. No matter how bright your future might be, if you are not looking within and looking to address patterns, you are in danger of repeating destructive behavior.

Lastly, I'd like you to list five positive behaviors that you can aspire to live out starting today. Think what you want reflected back to you whether it is from friends, family, or a partner.

Write them in present tense. Consider placing this list on a Post-it note somewhere you see it every day. Bathroom mirrors and car dashboards work great.

For example:

1. I am going to smile at each person I pass each day because a smile is contagious.

2. I will be honest with family and friends about my feelings when I've had a bad day.

I will share what attributes I love about my friends and family, so they feel my love.

GRATITUDE PRACTICE

"Breathe. Let go. And remind yourself that this very moment is the only one you know you have for sure."

—Oprah Winfrey

"Symbols are powerful because they are the visible signs of invisible realities."

—Saint Augustine

12

Spiritual Signs of the Times

How can you keep your head up and search for happiness without denying yourself the need to feel what you need to feel? This is a real question and there is not an easy answer.

Even when it hurt like hell, I continued to search for joy. I know this may sound over simplified. It's not.

Let's just take the physical aspect of this idea.

Standing outside, you look down, you see your feet and a circumference of say, 4 feet around you and a 180-degree span. You begin to walk down a path in the woods. It is important to look down and watch where your feet are going and to avoid obstacles such as tree roots, rocks, puddles and possibly holes in the ground.

Now you begin to walk down the path and you look up. You look side to side; you can turn your head 360 degrees just with a few steps. You have increased your perspective. You can now see a thorny branch sticking out. You can see the flowers that are blooming along the path. You can see a bench up ahead where you can rest.

Now, let's look up — way up into the sky. You see a tree branch with a bird's nest and a mother bird flying to find food for her baby birds. You see a plane traveling to an unknown place. You see clouds in motion on their way across the country.

There is no limit to what you can see. Right?

Let's take a look at each of these views or perspectives in a relationship sense.

The Safe Place

When someone is not letting the world in or not putting themselves out in the world, this is the "head down" phase. Many of us, especially in times of pain or sorrow, go within ourselves, our homes, or our relationships. If we isolate ourselves, it can be dangerous because when we have our head down, it is almost impossible to find our way out.

When I was in this place, I stopped going to church where I had been very involved. I started running by myself instead of with a group or a friend. I was not telling anyone how unhappy I was. I was ashamed that my world was so screwed up. I was just surviving because holding together my broken heart took all the energy I had. I had hardly anything to give — or so I thought.

Yes, there is a time and place in all of our lives to feel like and live like this. It's called self-preservation and we all have instincts that fire and tell us to go to a safe place.

There is nothing wrong with you if you find yourself here. It is just a season of life where your soul is preparing for the next steps.

The Horizon

Once you begin to feel the need to escape this place of isolation, your heart and mind are showing you that you are stuck in a place where you cannot grow. You begin to feel an overwhelming urge to scan the horizon and look for a place to go, to be, to breathe.

I believe this means you have grown stronger. Your soul is telling you it's time.

I felt this when I finally realized how trapped I'd felt and how long I'd felt that way. I'd been fighting so hard to save my marriage, I had completely lost myself. But once this reality became apparent, I needed to scan the horizon. I needed to reconnect with my friends and family. I needed their support.

I began to seek out friends I believed would see the broken me, hold me up and help me find the next steps. God, I don't know what I would have done without their vision of who I was and who I could be. They could see my strength, my resilience and my drive even when I had forgotten that innate part of me.

"One day at a time," they would say.

"One minute at a time," I thought.

The mentality had already been something I practiced. When training for a half-marathon with my daughter, we used interval training. I told her what I said to myself to keep pushing through in the later miles. I said, "I can do anything for one minute."

Now I needed to apply that resiliency to getting myself unstuck.

You too, with or without friends, have the ability to pull out of the tough places, out of your hole, out of your own head.

Your heart can heal and the sooner you believe that, the sooner it will begin to happen.

It likely will be a long path to walk down to find peace and wholeness, much less joy. But it is a path worth traveling because it is such a beautiful place at the end of this path. This place is called peace.

EMPOWERMENT PRACTICE 12: WALKING MEDITATION FOR PERSPECTIVE

I want to take you back to the beginning of the chapter when I had you visualize walking down a path. We are going to take a walk.

If at all possible, the first part of this exercise should be done outside on a flat safe area preferably a walking path. If that is not possible, the hallway of a building or a gymnasium would work. The second part of the exercise will be done in your workshop or if you can create a nest — that works too!

If you would like to remove distractions because the area is noisy, feel free to use headphones or earbuds. But what I recommend you do is put on white noise or use a sound machine to provide a soothing noise such as running water.

Part 1: Perspective Walk

1. Think about one thing that is holding you back right now. Give it a name of no more than three words and use past tense if possible. For example: “I wasn’t confident” or “I was lonely.”

   While walking about 100 yards at a casual pace looking down at your feet, repeat those three words slowly. Keep your feet moving and your head down as your perspective. Don’t turn your head or look around unless it is necessary for safety. Note what you are seeing as you walk because you will write this down later.

2. If safe, close your eyes and stand still. Safety first though! While counting to five, slowly take a big breath in. Now breathe it out counting to five. Do this five times. Relax your shoulders, your arms, shake out your legs.

3. Now think of something in your life that is positive and brings you joy. Name it in three words in present tense. For example: "I am growing" or "I love music" or "Talking to children"

   Now walk another 100 yards at a casual pace looking ahead while repeating your joyful words. This time you may turn your head side to side. Take in what you are seeing because later I will ask you to write this down.

4. If safe, close your eyes and stand still. While counting to five, slowly take in a big breath. Now breathe it out counting to five. Do this five times. Relax your shoulders, your arms, shake out your legs.

5. Find a place where you can see the sky, preferably not under a tree or next to a big building. If you are inside, you will close your eyes and use your imagination here.

   Think of something you want in your future life that you feel is missing. Name it in a few words and use present tense. For example: "I'm in love" or "I'm grateful" or "Walking the beach."

Stand with your feet hip distance apart. Take in a deep breath raising your arms over your head. Spread your fingers wide and reach for the sky. As you breathe out, lower your arms. If you are inside, close your eyes but still look up and imagine clouds floating overhead and the infinite blue sky.

6. Now very slowly turn in a circle five times or walk in a circle if possible, keeping your eyes on the sky and repeating your words. Smile while you are doing this. Feel your body moving, see the infinite sky, imagine a kite flying above or a plane soaring overhead.

   Remember to note what you saw in this perspective.

7. If safe, close your eyes. While counting to five, slowly take a big breath in. Now breathe it out counting to five. Do this five times. Relax your shoulders, your arms, shake out your legs. Smile!

Part 2: Remembrance

Go to a safe place, hopefully your workshop or nest. Bring pen and paper or open a blank document on your computer.

1. Write down your thoughts from Part 1 when your head was down.

   - How did you feel repeating those words while walking?

- What did you see? Did you feel restricted?
- How did it feel to breathe afterward?

2. Write down your thoughts from perspective 2 when you could look up and around.

    - How did you feel repeating your joyful words? Did you smile?

    - What did you see as you looked around? Did you feel more free?

    - How did it feel to breathe afterward this time? Was it different?

3. Write down your thoughts from perspective 3 when you were looking up and reaching for the sky.

    - How did you feel repeating your future hopes while looking up?

    - What did you see as you looked up? Did you feel hopeful, free or challenged?

    - How did it feel to breathe afterward? Was it different?

If you ever feel stuck, come back to this exercise. Use it to free your mind and breathe.

GRATITUDE PRACTICE

"When you are grateful, fear disappears, and abundance appears."

—Tony Robbins

"First best is falling in love. Second best is being in love. Least best is falling out of love. But any of it is better than never having been in love."

—Maya Angelou

13

Let's Talk Relationships

As we begin the chapter on relationships, I first want to say thank you for coming on this ride with me. It's been a process for me to walk through the details of my living, loving and losing, and then growing and gaining.

My friend Kaye said to me that writing The Swipe Right Effect was me fulfilling the need to use my pain for good. That's a beautiful way to look at the process I've walked through, and my hope is that you are helped by the information that helped me.

Another friend Crystal shared with me a quote by Duke basketball coach, Kara Lawson, from a speech to her team.

"... we all wait in life for things to get easier. I've just got to get through this, and life will be easier... It's what we do. We wait for stuff to get easier. It will never get easier.

What happens is you become someone that handles hard stuff better. So that's a mental shift that has to occur in each of our brains...

So, make yourself a person who handles the hard well. Not someone that's waiting on the easy. Because if you have a meaningful pursuit in life, it will never be easy....

So don't get discouraged through this time if it's hard. It's supposed to be. And don't wait for it to be easy. And whatever comes at you, you'll be great."

Tough words but oh, so true!

Now, when it comes to healing, sharing and vulnerability, not everyone is going to have the same capacity. As you've experienced change through the empowerment practices, you can feel an opening in your soul. Some people even describe feeling lighter as if a weight has been lifted.

It is a very personal choice to put yourself out into the world.

Relationships are defined in the Oxford language dictionary as:

"The way in which two or more concepts, objects, or people are connected, or the state of being connected."

Healthy relationships involve honesty, trust, respect and open communication between two or more people. Everyone needs to be willing to give and compromise and there should be no imbalance of power.

Whether you are married or dating, a relationship is where you make yourself vulnerable. Relationships are a place we can make mistakes; we can get hurt and we can see people at their worst.

And, yes, Coach Lawson, we also want it to get easier.

I have already walked through one of my worst nightmares but I'm hopeful and I'm strong. I'm not waiting for it to get easier because I've already learned how to do the hard stuff.

I handle hard things well now. And so can you!

All the single women you have met throughout the chapters of The Swipe Right Effect have agreed on one thing. Did you notice most had read and listened to Brené Brown?

You will make mistakes. And you need to give yourself grace. Think through the lessons to take from each experience and release it.

So now that you've done the hard work, let's take a look at who you are now. Let's see the new outline of who you are out in the world.

EMPOWERMENT PRACTICE 13:
WHO AM I AND HOW DO I IMPACT THE WORLD?

You have been doing a lot of hard things while going through this workbook. They are hard things and hopefully you are getting good at doing the hard things.

Below are prompts for you to work through that will give you some clarity on who you are at this moment and how you want to impact the world and be seen by the world. I think the questions have high value whether you are a mentor, a friend, a boss, or a parent. Think through what you have learned about yourself through the empowerment practices and put it to use for yourself.

I want you to see YOU through another's eyes for all the beautiful ways you brighten the world.

What can you show the world about how special you are, what you have to offer and what brings you joy? How can you openly share your gifts, skills, values and energy with others?

Whether you are dating or not, have fun with this and if you use your answers on a profile, I wish you the best. Go have fun!

20 Questions:
What the World Gets to Know About Me

1. About me in 100 words or less.

2. My interests are:

3. Relationships I want in my life include:

4. To me, a happy relationship looks like:

5. My friends say I am:

6. The world is a great place because:

7. When we hang out, I'd like to:

8. Never have I ever:

9. My ideal day is:

10. This year I really want to:

11. You can make me laugh by:

12. I get along best with people who:

13. My love languages are:

14. I love to relax by:

15. My greatest strength is:

16. My vision for my future includes:

17. I can impact on those around me when I:

18. A few things I had to let go to be happy:

19. What I hold to be true about myself:

20. My legacy to the world will be:

GRATITUDE PRACTICE

"Gratitude, like faith, is a muscle. The more you use it, the stronger it grows, and the more power you have to use it on your behalf. If you do not practice gratefulness, its benefaction will go unnoticed, and your capacity to draw on its gifts will be diminished. To be grateful is to find blessings in everything. This is the most powerful attitude to adopt, for there are blessings in everything."

—Alan Cohen

About the Author

C.K. Collins, aka Kelly, writes about her empowering five-year journey back to joy, happiness and love. Her inner healing has been a grassroots effort, surrounded by supportive friends and family, who held her hand, shared her pain and hugged her through a lot of tough moments following a traumatic divorce.

In gratitude and recognition of the gifts of love she has received, Kelly unfolds her ongoing journey to wholeness through storytelling and shares the lessons she learned from her friends all over the world.

Kelly owned her own company in the news publishing business and after she sold it, she took a two-year sabbatical. She is diving into writing books that empower people walking the tough path of loss. She believes that gratitude, empathy and love are the recipe for a fruitful and joyful life.

She originally hails from Tennessee and currently lives in the Northeast US. She has been traveling the world as often as possible. Her next books will include stories and lessons from her adventures and the amazing shifts in perspective acquired through solo travel.

With her beloved daughters is where she feels most wholly loved and seen.

WE WANT TO HEAR

YOUR STORY

GO TO

MySwipeRightStory.com

I'd love to hear your story of resilience, courage and vulnerability.

@CKCOLLINSAUTHOR. |. CKCOLLINS.CO

Made in the USA
Columbia, SC
13 September 2023

22831655R00072